Easy Concertos and Concertinos
for Violin and Piano

H. Millies

Concertino
in D

in the style of Mozart

(1st position)

Bosworth

CONCERTINO

im Stil von W. A. Mozart (1756-1791)

I. POSITION

In the style of W. A. Mozart - Dans le style de W. A. Mozart

Hans Millies

8

Andante

Easy Concertos and Concertinos
for Violin and Piano

H. Millies

Concertino
in D

in the style of Mozart

(1st position)

Bosworth

CONCERTINO
im Stil von W. A. Mozart (1756-1791)
I. POSITION

In the style of W. A. Mozart / Dans le style de W. A. Mozart

g. B. = mit dem ganzen Bogen- Whole Bow- Tout l'archet
u. H. = mit der unteren Hälfte des Bogens- Lower Half of the Bow- Moitié inférieure de l'archet
o. H. = mit der oberen Hälfte des Bogens- Upper Half of the Bow- Moitié supérieure de l'archet
M. = mit der Mitte- In the Middle- Au milieu
Sp. = an der Spitze- At the Tip- À la pointe
Fr. = am Frosch- At the nut- Au talon
simile = ähnlich, ebenso, d. h. das Folgende so spielen wie das Vorhergehende
= "like" i. e. play the following in the same way as the preceding
= semblable c. a. d. interpréter cette partie de la même manière que la précédente
‒‒‒‒ = breite (geschobene) Striche- Broad bowing- Largement détaché
· · · · = geworfene Striche (und Springbogen)- Spiccato (and springing)- Jeté (et sautillé)
⸗⸗⸗⸗ = fest gestoßene Striche- Detached- Coups détachés ferme

Hans Millies

Andante

Rondo

Allegretto

Printed and bound in Great Britain by
Caligraving Limited Thetford Norfolk

Rondo

Allegretto

un poco più tranquillo

B. & Co., 20471